HIGH-TECH CRIME FIGHTERS

Crime Busters
by Lou Ann Walker

Clues from the Lab
by Andra Serlin

GLOBE FEARON

Pearson Learning Group

Contents

Crime Busters

Clues from the Lab

Crime BUSTERS

by Lou Ann Walker

CHAPTER 1

Beyond a Reasonable Doubt

You've just walked onto the scene of a crime. What questions pop into your head? Do you think about what happened there? Who committed the crime? Why did it happen?

Now imagine that you are a government prosecutor. It is your job to send the criminal to jail. Of course, you want the right person to be convicted of the crime. Once you have a suspect, the **pivotal** question for you would be: How can your theories about the crime be proved? That's where "forensics" comes in.

Forensics is the use of science and technology to investigate an event, usually a crime. Forensic science is often used to investigate cases in which violence has occurred, such as assault, kidnapping, or murder. However, forensics is also used in nonviolent crimes, such as identity theft and forgery. A forensic scientist is often a detective. He or she must gather and examine clues. A forensic scientist works to unravel the details surrounding a crime. Even the cleverest criminal can sometimes be identified by the use of forensics.

It's the job of law enforcement officials to arrest criminals. Then, they must convince judges and juries "beyond a reasonable doubt" that the right person was arrested. **According** to this principle, the judge and jurors must be fairly confident, based on the evidence, that the accused person is guilty.

The work of forensic scientists begins with collecting evidence at the crime scene. Forensic scientists examine the crime scene along with the police.

Investigators must be careful not to upset anything at a crime scene. They must make sure nothing new is added. Every possible piece of evidence is photographed or videotaped before it can be taken away.

At a crime scene, investigators search for all the clues involved with the crime. They dust for fingerprints. They scrape up small bits of evidence using scalpels. Small, angled mirrors, like the ones dentists have, are used to see beneath heavy furniture. Tweezers are used to pick up fibers. Of course, investigators must be **consistent** when labeling where each piece of evidence was found before it can be stored in a bag.

The evidence is then sent to forensic labs. At these labs, scientists **administer** tests to determine whether the evidence is connected to the crime.

The field of forensics is exploding. New techniques are helping forensic scientists to solve more crimes each year. Also, there are many new forensic areas, or **domains**, such as computer forensics. A forensic scientist in any specialty might be asked to provide **factual** information about a case at any time.

Forensic scientists look for answers to questions about how a crime occurred. Imagine how exciting it must be to finally solve a case, to find the answer to something you have puzzled over. Finding answers is the job—and the ultimate reward—of a forensic scientist.

A forensic scientist must carefully examine evidence at a crime scene. How do you think the information he finds helps to solve a crime?

CHAPTER 2

One in a Million

There aren't always witnesses to a crime. Besides, witnesses are not always reliable. They may be scared or confused. So, how can law enforcement officials identify suspects? A suspect can be identified when features unique to the suspect place him or her at a crime scene.

Hands-on Evidence

Do you see loops and swirls on your fingertips? These patterns, or fingerprints, are unique to you. Each of us has a unique pattern of marks on our hands and feet.

Fingerprints were first used as **factual** evidence in a Chicago court in 1910. A burglar left his prints on some wet paint. Today, criminals try not to leave that unique trace of themselves behind. They may wear gloves or wipe down surfaces. Forensic scientists have had to become very clever at **obtaining** fingerprints.

Early fingerprint comparisons were made when scientists gathered easily seen prints. Soon, researchers realized that invisible, or "latent," prints made by sweat could be found on many surfaces. Latent prints can last a long time. Some were even found in ancient tombs!

There are several ways to discover latent prints. One way is to dust with a special magnetic powder that sticks to the prints. Another technique uses clear tape to "lift," or pick up, prints.

Some types of surfaces require different techniques for uncovering fingerprints. For example, scientists can press specially treated paper against a victim's skin. The paper can pick up fingerprints possibly left by a criminal. However, fingerprints on skin rarely last for more than about 2 hours.

If the prints are on wood or cardboard, the item is sprayed with a special chemical. Then, the item is dried in an oven to make the prints appear. If the area to be searched is large, finding fingerprints can be hard. Sometimes, a chemical found in super-strong glue is sprayed in a sealed room. This chemical makes any prints show up white.

Laser beams can also reveal latent prints. Wearing tinted goggles in the laboratory, the scientist focuses the laser beam on an object such as a gun. The U.S. Department of Justice used a laser beam to help confirm that a man had been a Nazi guard during World War II. How was his past uncovered? Using a laser beam, scientists revealed the man's thumbprint on a postcard he'd sent to a top Nazi official.

Hiding the Prints

Some criminals have gone to great lengths to hide their prints. One burglar wore surgical gloves when he broke into a post office in England. However, once outside, he tore off the gloves and left them behind. Law-enforcement officials were able to lift his prints from inside the gloves. One criminal had a doctor remove the skin on his fingertips. However, the special ridge pattern on the rest of his fingers gave him away.

In 1990, a Miami drug dealer was arrested. His hands were cut up and bleeding. To hide his identity, the man had sliced his fingertips. An FBI agent photographed the dealer's damaged fingers. He then spent weeks rearranging the lines to look the way nature had made them. The result was a match with fingerprints from another drug case.

DNA: A New Kind of Fingerprint

Whenever you sip water from a glass, you leave a bit of yourself behind—not just your fingerprints, but also DNA from your saliva. Like fingerprints, our DNA is completely unique to us. The only exception is identical twins. What if an identical twin commits a crime? How would investigators find the right twin? Surprisingly, the answer is fingerprints. Although identical twins share the same DNA, their fingerprints are different. Fingerprint patterns form slightly differently in every person while developing inside the womb.

One British scientist claims that the possibility of two people who are not related having the same DNA pattern is less than 1 in—get ready for a big number—1 nonillion. This is a 1 with 30 zeroes after it. That's far more than the number of people living on Earth today!

Everyone's DNA has the same basic chemical structure. Human DNA contains four basic chemicals that are arranged in millions of pairs. It is the different arrangement of these pairs that makes every person's DNA unique.

Every cell in a person's body is **consistent** in having the same DNA. We leave behind that DNA whenever we lick a stamp, cry, or wear a baseball cap.

In the past, scientists needed about 150 cells to make a DNA match. Today, they need only about 6. That's how many cells might be left inside a ski mask or in a fingerprint smudge.

As a test, scientists at one New York City crime lab actually broke into each other's apartments. They wanted to see if they would leave enough DNA for analysis. They were trying not to leave any traces of themselves behind. The experiment proved that the new techniques worked. They could identify each other from tiny samples of fingerprints, sweat, and hair.

How do you think investigators **obtain** DNA samples? At the scene of a crime, they look for hairs with the root still attached. They look for skin cells, or blood and other bodily fluids. They look for licked envelopes or baseball caps. Even a lost tooth contains DNA. Once investigators have a suspect, they may take a swab of the cells inside the suspect's cheek. That swab, with the cells on it, is then sealed in a plastic tube. The sample is kept from becoming contaminated.

DNA is also used to determine whether or not two people are related. People who are related have similar DNA. In England in the 1990s, archaeologists found a skull from a prehistoric man in a cave. The scientists wondered whether or not the man's descendants lived in the area. They asked children from the local school to give blood. The blood was compared to the DNA taken from the skull. The children's DNA did not match that of the prehistoric man. However, the man turned out to be an ancestor of a teacher!

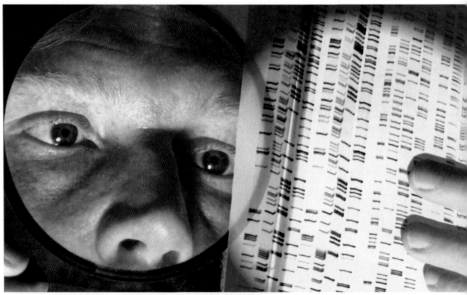

This forensic scientist is comparing DNA samples. It is highly unlikely that two people, except for identical twins, can have the same DNA information.

Some of the early techniques for matching DNA were not very reliable. Some DNA cases were thrown out of court. The technicians just couldn't be sure that the correct person was on trial.

However, DNA evidence has helped prove the innocence of many people who were wrongly accused. In 1987, police in England were trying to solve a case by using DNA. They took blood samples from 5,000 men in the area. None of the samples matched those from the crime scene. A janitor at a local psychiatric hospital confessed to the crime. He was arrested, but his confession was full of errors and **inconsistencies**.

By chance, someone mentioned that a man in town had paid another person to give a blood sample for him. When the police heard this news, they realized that the wrong person might be behind bars. They took DNA from both the jailed suspect and the man who had given someone else's blood. Sure enough, the janitor who had been arrested was innocent. The other man's DNA helped prove him guilty of the crime.

Bloodstains on clothing must be carefully analyzed. DNA studies can reveal whether the blood is from a victim or a suspect.

Serious DNA studies began in the 1980s. They quickly showed their usefulness. Many countries around the world now have DNA databases. In the 1990s, the Combined DNA Index System, or CODIS, was introduced in the United States. CODIS was created and is currently **administered** by the Federal Bureau of Investigation (FBI). The DNA information it contains is shared with other law-enforcement agencies.

By 2004, CODIS had been used in more than 16,600 investigations. Of that number, CODIS had come up with 13,600 "hits." In other words, the system has helped to solve 13,600 cases. It is extremely **productive**.

Today, a number of "cold cases" are being solved using DNA. Cold cases are unsolved crimes. Police departments in many U.S. cities are able to reopen unsolved crime files and reinvestigate what happened. New York City set up a cold case unit in 1996. Within four years, it had solved almost a third of its unsolved cases, leading to 295 arrests.

Why are cold case investigations today so successful? Earlier DNA samples had to be large and in excellent condition. As we've seen, samples can be smaller and less well preserved today.

Solving these cold cases is important to victims and their families. It allows them to feel that they can finally move on with their lives after their difficult experience.

Another important program involving DNA is known as the Human Genome Project. The goal of this program is to map the complete human genome, or DNA code. British law-enforcement officers are making a surprising prediction. They say that by using the DNA from a crime scene and the human genome, they will soon be able to issue a complete description of a suspect. Imagine being able to create a near-exact drawing of someone from just a drop of sweat!

CHAPTER 3

Blood, Sweat, Tears, and More

Bodily fluids, such as blood, offer many more secrets than just a person's identity. Certain tests of those fluids can be very **productive**. They can tell us, for example, what poisons, drugs, or other foreign substances are in a body.

Rust, dried shoe polish, and dried fruit juice can look just like dried blood. Investigators must have no **lingering** doubts that the spots they see at a crime scene are, indeed, bloodstains. Using an eyedropper, technicians place a few drops of a certain chemical onto a spot. If another type of chemical found in blood is present, the substance will show pink and foam up.

Another test can determine whether the blood **obtained** is human or animal. Scientists use a gel-coated glass slide with two grooves in it. They add a special chemical to one groove. Then, they add a drop of blood to the other groove. Finally, they pass a mild electric current over the slide. If the liquids move toward each other, then the blood is from an animal rather than a human.

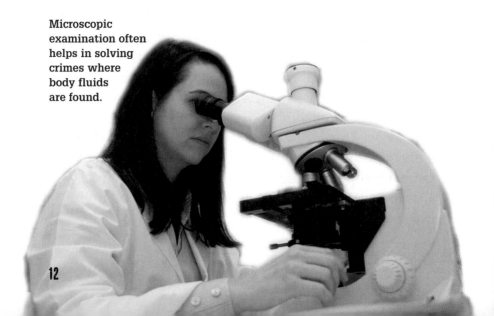

Microscopic examination often helps in solving crimes where body fluids are found.

Drops of Blood

The average adult body contains about 10 pints of blood. Much of this blood may be lost during a violent crime. The way the blood is **dispersed** can offer important clues to investigators.

In the 1930s, a Scottish scientist named John Glaister noted that there are different types of blood splashes that can occur when a victim has been hit by a heavy object. Blood drops that fall directly down to a horizontal surface are somewhat round. The size and shape of the drops indicate from what height the blood has fallen. Blood drops appear more and more crown-shaped the farther they have to fall. Drops that fly through the air will hit the horizontal surface at an angle. The resulting splash marks show which way the blood traveled.

Even when a major blood vessel is cut, a person's heart continues pumping. This **exertion** causes the blood to spurt. Blood spurts can reach the ceiling and are likely to hit the person who caused the injury. If there is a pool of blood around a victim, the person died at that location. Blood trails show that a body was moved or carried.

If there are many tiny drops, then the blood traveled at very high speeds, perhaps as a result of a gunshot. Medium-sized drops mean that the weapon was probably a knife or a blunt object. Fewer, bigger drops show that the weapon was perhaps a fist.

A crime scene investigator measures how far blood has traveled and the size of bloodstains. Photographs of blood spatters must **consistently** include objects of known size, such as a pencil or a coin. Including these objects helps to show the relative size of the drops.

Finding Hidden Traces

Of course, many criminals **exert** great effort to clean up bloodstains after a violent crime. Investigators check whether bleach had been used recently or whether one area appears to be cleaner than another. If so, someone might have been trying to get rid of **factual** evidence. To find traces of blood, forensic scientists start by shining a very bright light over all the surfaces at a crime scene.

Sometimes, the bright light doesn't reveal blood traces. Investigators might still suspect that a crime was involved. If so, they spray a chemical called luminol over surfaces. Luminol is very sensitive to blood. In fact, it can detect a single drop of blood in a container of 999,999 drops of water. Seconds after the luminol has been sprayed, crime scene investigators turn out all the lights. Luminol glows green-blue everywhere that it comes in contact with blood. It will glow even if that blood is years old.

Hema sticks are also used to find traces of blood. A hema stick is shaped like an ice-pop stick. It has a blood-sensitive chemical on one end. Investigators touch the treated end to a stained surface; then they spray that end with distilled water. Back in the laboratory, they can determine if human blood is on the hema stick.

Investigators can also look for saliva and other bodily fluids by spraying surfaces with a protein. This protein makes fluids glow when a laser is shined on them.

No matter what type of bodily fluid is found, a comparison microscope will probably be used to analyze it. When using a comparison microscope, two slides can be examined at the same time through one eyepiece. Another very important tool is the electron microscope. This instrument can magnify objects up to a million times.

Death by Poisoning

In addition to the microscope, scientists in a laboratory rely on a centrifuge. A centrifuge is a cylinder that spins 2,000 to 3,000 times per minute. When researchers suspect poisoning or a drug overdose, they add a chemical to the blood to be tested. Then, they spin the mixture in the centrifuge. The poison or drug and chemical rise to the top. The blood, which is heavier, sinks to the bottom.

To identify a poison or drug separated by the centrifuge, forensic scientists then coat a glass slide with a gel. They dab the end of the slide with the unidentified substance. Then, they dip this end into a special liquid. The liquid rises up through the gel. As the liquid rises, it carries with it beads of the different components. The beads are compared to charts that help identify the substances present. This same laboratory technique is important for many other forensic studies. For example, people living near waste dumps can use it to find out if the water they drink contains toxic chemicals.

Death by poisoning can be determined by using a centrifuge. This centrifuge spins around 50 times a second to separate chemicals from bodily fluids.

Telltale Teeth

Picture finding a single tooth. You wouldn't think that teeth could offer much information, would you? However, teeth often provide excellent clues to the mysteries that a detective must solve.

One reason these body parts are so useful is that they last for a very long time after death. Teeth are nearly impossible to destroy. When there is a disaster, such as an airplane crash or a fire, 85 percent of the time investigators rely on dental records to identify bodies.

After the New York City World Trade Center attacks in 2001, volunteers from the New York Mass Disaster Dental Forensics Team worked for months. As each unidentified individual was found, forensic dental workers compared teeth to dental records. Being able to identify people after a tragedy is important for families and forensic workers as well. "Returning victims to their families is the most consoling aspect of this work," said Winnie Furnari, a volunteer **coordinator**.

Teeth offer lots of **productive** information. They can show the approximate age of a person by the amount of enamel and the thickness of the enamel on the teeth. Most people go regularly to a dentist. The dentist records every filling, bridge, and peculiarity of the mouth. Having such records makes the forensic dentist's job much easier.

Dental records are also used when there is a bite mark. Bite marks are important in some child abuse cases as well as in some other violent crimes. Forensic workers take a color photograph of a bite mark as soon as possible. A ruler is included in the frame for size comparison.

Sometimes, forensic scientists use ultraviolet (UV) light. Although the eye might not detect a bite-mark pattern, UV light can reveal it months after the person was bitten. A suspect is then asked to bite into a waxlike material to make a cast of his or her teeth. When the cast is made, it is compared to the victim's bite-mark pattern. Bite marks were first allowed into evidence in England in 1906. At that time, a burglar foolishly took a bite of cheese at a crime scene. His hunger gave him away!

Human bites in victims can cause serious injuries. Did you know that when a dog bites a person, there's a 2 to 20 percent chance of infection? When a human bites a human, there's a 10 to 50 percent chance!

Bone-Chilling Facts

Imagine looking at a few bones and being able to tell the age, race, and sex of a person. For example, men have heavier skulls than women and a bony ridge on the forehead. Women have wider pelvic bones.

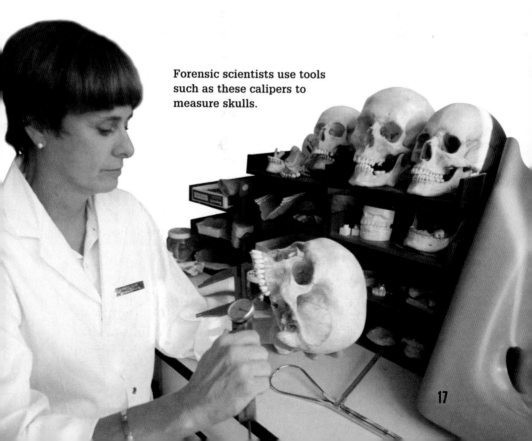

Forensic scientists use tools such as these calipers to measure skulls.

Bones can also tell a story to investigators by the texture of their surface. Muscles are attached to bones when a person is alive. The muscles decay after death. If a bone's surface is rough, investigators know that the person had overused the muscles attached. By looking at a female skeleton with rough, grainy shoulder ridges on her right side, forensic investigators were able to **devise** a theory that the woman had been a waitress. She probably carried a lot of heavy dishes and balanced them on her right side.

In one amazing case, a doctor looked at just three different human bones to solve a murder. There were two bones from the hip and one from the back. By taking some measurements, the doctor figured out that the bones had belonged to a young woman. From the grooving he found in the hip bones, he could tell that she'd had a baby. There was also a bullet in one hip. From the bullet hole, he saw that the right hip was bigger than the left. From these clues he could tell that she was short and slim, had polio as a child, and limped when she walked. He could also tell that she had been killed by a shotgun from about 9 feet away.

When the local police asked around, they discovered that a 24-year-old woman who had a baby was missing. The woman was divorced and had gone home to live with her father. Her father had been cleaning his gun one day when it went off. He'd tried to save his daughter's life. However, she had died anyway. He then buried her without telling the police.

Another strange case involved a female skull that was found in 1983 in a swamplike area in England. Afterward, a man went to the police. He confessed that he'd killed his wife more than twenty years before. However, when the skull was tested, it was found to be more than 1,700 years old!

Splitting Hairs

Like teeth, hair also lasts a long time. Hairs from various parts of the body look different under a microscope. Hair from the top of the head is round. Beard hairs are usually triangular. Eyebrow and eyelash hairs are circular but have tapered tips.

Giving hair samples isn't much fun. Investigators may pluck as many as 100 hairs from a suspect's head. They look for different shadings of color and different hair structures.

Hair from a beard can be easily identified. The tip of each hair has a triangular shape.

If someone has been poisoned, the poison may show up in the hair. To find poisons such as thallium, arsenic, or antimony, investigators put the victim's hair into wax to keep it from moving. Then, they study the hair under a microscope.

Evidence of hairs and fibers are often hard to find. Investigators have to use a very strong light. They also have to look at floor surfaces. Hairs and fibers take time to settle in a room or car trunk. Police say that criminals may sometimes return to a crime scene. However, forensic investigators must always return for another look!

CHAPTER 4

What's Real and What Isn't

In the early 1980s, a German magazine called *Stern* paid $2.3 million for 62 notebooks supposedly written by Nazi leader Adolph Hitler. The magazine had asked experts to compare the diary entries with samples of Hitler's handwriting. The experts said the notebooks were definitely written by Hitler.

There was excitement all over the world about these documents. The West German government was skeptical, though. It asked forensic specialists to test the paper, glue, and ink.

Experts discovered that the paper contained a chemical that had not been used in paper before 1954. Hitler had died nine years before that date. The ink was also tested. After the tests, there were no **lingering** doubts. The documents couldn't have been **authentic**. They had been written less than a year before.

The person who had written the diaries was a master forger. The handwriting experts had been fooled because they were comparing the diaries to other forgeries by the same man! Only the chemists could be sure.

Counterfeiting money is one of history's oldest crimes. In early times, it was punishable by death. Today, more than $130 million in counterfeit U.S. bills are in circulation. The U.S. Secret Service has a Forensic Services Division (FSD). This group analyzes documents, credit cards, and paper money to find out what is real and what is fake.

Computers and printers have become very advanced. Counterfeiters today are very good at what they do. The federal government had to find a way to protect its money. That's why its paper money, which is 25 percent linen and 75 percent cotton, was recently changed. It now includes holograms and other elements that are very difficult to duplicate. A hologram is a laser-created image. Often, people can just feel the difference in the money. Many counterfeiters use cheap paper. Others bleach $1 bills and then print pictures of $100 bills on them.

Accordingly, the Secret Service has worked with different groups to expose large counterfeiting operations. In one case, it teamed up with Colombian officials. Together, they found a fully equipped room to make counterfeit money beneath a banana plantation. From the style of money found there, forensic scientists determined that more than $20 million in bills had been made in that one room during a 10-year period.

Secret Service Snooping

Forensic chemists are hired by the Secret Service to spot counterfeit bills. One set of tests involves trying to find out what kind of tree the paper came from. Dogs also play a **pivotal** role in chemical forensic tests. The Secret Service trains them to sniff out the foreign chemicals used in making counterfeit bills.

The Secret Service also has its own document examiners. These forensic specialists study counterfeit checks, postage stamps, treasury bonds, and food stamps. One of the most important tasks in forensics is keeping up with the latest technologies for making illegal copies, or forgeries, of paintings and other works of fine art.

Writing Tools That Tell All

Believe it or not, there is a library that has only one thing in it—ink—7,000 kinds of ink. Called the International Ink Library, it is **administered** by the Secret Service. Forensic investigators use the library collection to find out the brand and kind of ink that was used on a sheet of paper. As was the case with the Hitler diaries, they often need to know the earliest possible date a certain type of ink was made.

The Secret Service also has a watermark collection. A watermark is a design pressed onto paper when it is made. Ordinary copy paper does not have a watermark. However, many kinds of stationery do have watermarks. To find out if a sheet of paper has a watermark, hold it up to a light. Look carefully for a design. The Secret Service has 22,000 designs in its watermark collection. These designs are **pivotal** for finding out when and where a sheet of paper was made.

Sometimes, there are changes on a document that weren't intended by its creators. These changes may not be obvious to the naked eye. Forensic scientists often use infrared photography to detect these changes.

Infrared photography uses infrared radiation to take pictures. Infrared radiation is invisible to the human eye. However, this type of radiation is detected by humans as heat. Infrared photography was **devised** to capture that invisible radiation and show it on film.

Infrared photographs can show how documents have been altered when everything looks normal to the naked eye. Infrared photography, though very useful, is tricky to use. It requires a special lens filter on the camera. The film must be kept in cold storage. However, it must be at room temperature when the photograph is taken. Also, the film must be loaded and unloaded in darkness.

FISHing for Information

It's a serious crime to forge other people's names on wills, checks, or contracts. Investigators work slowly and carefully, trying to uncover the work of criminals who are trying to illegally match other people's handwriting. In a kidnapping, however, a criminal is more often trying to disguise, not copy, handwriting. Experts must work fast to figure out who wrote the ransom note.

The Secret Service **devised** the Forensic Information System for Handwriting, or FISH. Using FISH, investigators can enter samples of handwriting into a computer database. Then, using the giant database, they compare a written sample to other handwritten documents. FISH can help solve kidnapping cases and cases of threats against public figures. FISH is available to investigators all over the United States.

U.S. paper money is the most popular type of currency to be counterfeited. It is also the easiest type of paper money to counterfeit.

Reading Between the Lines

Everyone's handwriting is unique. For example, some of us have quirks in the way we make the letter *m* or *k*. For fun, people may try to analyze someone's handwriting in order to make guesses about his or her personality. Forensic scientists may do this, too. More often, though, they study handwriting to try to figure out who wrote something, or if someone was trying to disguise his or her handwriting.

Investigators need large samples of someone's handwriting to compare to a database of handwriting samples. Getting a large sample, though, isn't always possible. Most notes that robbers give when they rob a bank, for example, are short. "Put the money in the bag," is a sample. The amount of writing isn't much for the handwriting expert to go on.

The experts also look for small clues. For example, they look at the way a person has held the pen or pencil. If a person is writing something that isn't true, he or she will tend to lift the pen from the paper more. The experts look at the smoothness of each line. A person's handwriting changes if he or she is scared, sick, or under stress. The lines are jagged and more at an angle.

When you hear people speak, you can often tell if they're from the southern or the northern parts of the United States. The same is true with the way people write. For example, people in the Midwest might use certain words in their writing that Californians might not use.

Linguists, people who study language, are an important part of document analysis. They **coordinate** with handwriting experts to find out where people come from. They also try to make guesses about a suspect's feelings and attitudes.

Read about the case of the Unabomber. This man made homemade bombs and sent them to people through the mail. The Unabomber also mailed to newspapers long articles he had written about his beliefs. He insisted that the newspapers print the articles or he would send more bombs. Linguists studied his words. They figured out many things about him. Surprisingly, it was the Unabomber's brother who called the police. He had read the letters in a newspaper and recognized the kind of language his brother used. The Unabomber was captured all because of the words and phrases he chose.

Paper Goods

A sheet of paper is just a sheet of paper, right? Not to investigators. You have already read about watermarks. There are plenty of other marks on paper that provide clues to tracking down the writer.

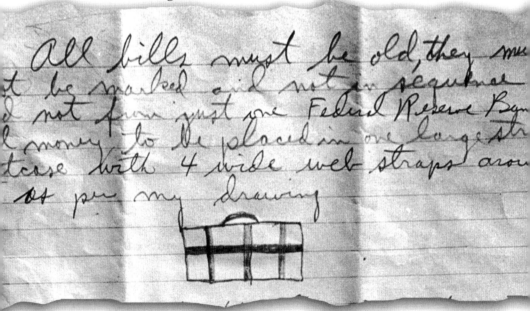

Styles of handwriting used in ransom or robbery notes can often reveal characteristics of the criminal.

A sheet of paper that was found at a crime scene had an impression of an anchor in one corner. Investigators found that it was from a button of a jacket. By further checking, they found out that the button was made for a uniform. They tracked down the company that made the uniform and where it was sold. This work helped investigators solve the case.

In another case, a woman was missing. Police found a notebook in her home. Investigators took UV photographs of the notebook. The notebook had the imprint of a lawn chair on it. However, the woman didn't own a lawn chair. The woman's boyfriend owned lawn chairs, though. The police began searching the boyfriend's house and soon found the woman's body.

The woman had been at the boyfriend's house with her notebook. He had killed the woman and then hidden her body. Then, he had brought the notebook back to the woman's house. He didn't want any traces of her in his own house from the day of the murder. When scientists took UV photographs of the notebook, the traces of the lawn chair matched the boyfriend's lawn chair. Case solved!

Often, a kidnapper will make many drafts when writing a ransom note. Investigators can find indentations on any paper that was beneath the final draft by using UV or infrared photography. They can also find impressions using devices that detect electrical charges in the paper.

Computer printers leave unique impressions and markings on paper as well. Each printer has its own quirks. A printer might have a scratch that leaves a distinctive mark on paper. Gears, belts, and rollers might leave marks as well. In addition, each toner fluid has a distinct chemical formula. A forensic chemist can **devise** tests that show where toner fluid came from.

Covering Up

Suppose you wanted to disguise your handwriting. How would you do it? Many people try to write with their opposite hand. However, people tire quickly when they are forced to write with the "wrong" hand. The writing becomes very sloppy.

Sometimes, to disguise their handwriting, men try to make their handwriting look more feminine. They may make circles over their *i*'s or big loops in letters. Women may do the opposite. They may press down hard on the paper and make more angles.

Criminals often create ransom notes made up of magazine or newspaper cutouts. Examiners compare the words or letters used with many different magazines and local newspapers across the country. Being able to identify the words or letters helps them to find out where the note was created.

The FBI's Questioned Documents Unit (QDU) keeps files of anonymous letters, bank robbery notes, as well as forged checks. This same unit keeps a running file of brand names and models of tires and shoes. When a tire or shoe print is discovered at a crime scene, investigators access this file. The file helps investigators to determine where the shoes or tires were made and bought.

Document experts need years of training. The FBI runs a two-year study program on methods and criminal psychology. This program is followed by hands-on training in the field. Further training may include practicing for courtroom appearances. Examiners have to be prepared to **clarify** every detail of their testimony. This training gets them ready for the tough cross-examinations they'll face in real courts of law.

Determining what is real and what is not is a tough job. Often, it takes years of training and experience to bring clever forgers and counterfeiters to justice.

CHAPTER 5

Using Art to Solve Crimes

Many criminals, including forgers, do more than try to disguise their handwriting when they are hiding from the law. They may dye their hair, cut it, or wear wigs. They may get tattoos or wear dark glasses in public. They may lose or gain weight. Some criminals on the loose may even use plastic surgery to change their appearance. That's when forensic artists can be most useful. Forensic artists use art techniques to assist law-enforcement officials in their investigations.

Framing Faces

Karen T. Taylor had a job illustrating road safety posters. A Texas Ranger came into her office in Texas one day and asked for her help. He'd heard that she was good at drawing faces. She'd acquired that skill when she did sculptures for a wax museum in London. The ranger brought Taylor to the home of an eight-year-old girl who had seen a hit-and-run driver injure the girl's young cousin. Taylor asked the girl many questions. Then, she drew a sketch of the driver. From Taylor's drawing, the Texas Rangers were able to find and arrest the driver of the car.

The ranger's request changed Taylor's life. It was the start of a fascinating career helping with criminal investigations, identifying victims, and locating lost children. Taylor says that her job is part artist and part psychologist. Over the years, she has developed certain interviewing techniques to **obtain** the information she needs to make her drawings. For example, she is careful not to upset the people she interviews while getting them to **clarify** and expand on what they remember.

Taylor does many "age-progression" drawings. If a child has been kidnapped and years have passed, then age-progression drawings try to show what the child would look like in the present. Forensic artists study how faces change as children grow, and they sketch their drawings **accordingly**.

Skull Sculpting

As adult fugitives age, they change, too. Sometimes, three-dimensional (3-D) representations are very useful. Using this technique, artists mold clay to make sculptures of heads based on how they think a person has aged. Any known scars or moles are included. In one famous case, a sculpture was shown on television 17 years after an adult male committed a crime. A woman recognized the face as belonging to that of a man who lived next door to her. She called the FBI. They arrested the fugitive a short time later.

Try to picture a case in which only a person's skull is found. A skull doesn't seem to be much to go on, does it? Forensic artists have to do some additional digging of their own. You'd be amazed at how much information can be **obtained** from the bare bones. The artist talks to scientists who are bone specialists. These people can tell from a bone's appearance what the person's ethnic background, sex, and approximate age might have been. By measuring the nasal opening, the artist can determine how wide the nose was. Even more can be learned from the space between the eye sockets, the height of the cheekbones, the length of the jaw, and the width of the forehead.

Once an artist has all that information, then he or she can determine how the skin and muscle tissue were stretched over the skull. Before making a clay model, an artist attaches short rods to a model skull. These rods indicate how deep the facial skin should be in those places. Then, the sculptor can contour the portrait head correctly.

Often, the dead body of a victim is so badly damaged or decayed that it cannot be identified. This deterioration can occur if a person has drowned, for example. Very often, forensic artists do post-mortem drawings. Police **disperse** these drawings to the public, to help them find out who the person was.

Throughout the 1980s and 1990s, Karen Taylor continued to try and make her representations of people even more **authentic**. In the 1990s, the FBI hired Taylor to teach other artists the skills she used in her forensic **domain**. Soon, she found herself being interviewed on television about her work. She has appeared on television programs such as *America's Most Wanted*. Her hands were seen molding a clay sculpture on the show *C.S.I.*

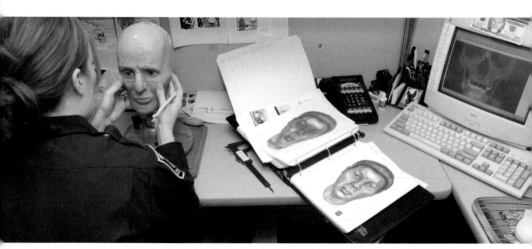

Forensic artists make sculptures to help identify victims or criminals.

Another technique Karen Taylor has pioneered is two-dimensional (2-D) facial reconstruction. When the body of a victim cannot be identified because of its poor condition, the head is x-rayed. Using Taylor's technique, the artist puts the x-ray on top of a box that has a light inside. The light helps the artist to examine the x-ray. He or she then marks the depth of facial tissue on the x-ray. Next, the artist puts a sheet of tracing paper on top of the x-ray. Using the markings, the artist draws a likeness of the deceased person's face.

One of the **limitations** of a drawing or a sculpture is its inability to show different facial expressions. Also, the representation can't show what people would look like under different lighting conditions. Today, forensic artists can use computer software to build a more lifelike three dimensional image of a person's head and face.

In one software program, the subject has 24 facial muscles that can actually move. With just a few keystrokes on the computer, people can gain or lose weight. Their hair can be styled differently. They can be shown smiling or looking angry. Although, the heads could be made to talk, they don't actually do any speaking. Forensic investigators believe that a talking head might confuse a witness.

No matter which artistic technique is used, artists must keep in mind the trauma that victims or witnesses have suffered. **Accordingly**, they must be very sensitive in deciding what questions to ask. At the same time, they must try to get descriptions that are as **factual** as possible.

Karen Taylor takes her work extremely seriously. To anyone who is thinking about a career as a forensic artist, she says, "The victims of violent crimes and the citizens whose lives your work may help safeguard deserve your full efforts."

CHAPTER 6

The Secrets in Bits and Bytes

Computers have helped investigators solve more crimes than ever before. Can you imagine police detectives trying to match one set of fingerprints to millions of others without a computer? Do you know that many computer databases that store information, such as DNA profiles, have helped to get rid of any **lingering** doubts about a person's guilt or innocence?

Surprisingly enough, computers have also opened up new ways for criminals to break the law. Hackers are computer users who gain unauthorized access to a computer system. Hackers can create havoc among the world's business and financial markets. Computer thieves don't have to wear masks. They simply steal money or goods electronically.

Each day, people **disperse** trillions of dollars around the world using computers. For example, they buy items online using credit cards. They do their banking on a computer. In doing these things, they are creating many opportunities for computer thieves. Maybe a computer doesn't seem to be as dangerous as a gun or a knife. However, it can cause plenty of trouble.

Cybercops on the Prowl

Forensic computer detectives may jokingly be called cybercops or digital sleuths. These investigators, though, have to be very good at what they do to capture Internet thieves and con artists.

To investigate a computer crime, computer forensic experts look at e-mail, online address books, and digital photographs. They also look at credit card activity— anything to help **clarify** how or why the crime took place. "Whenever we do a crime scene search, we plan on a computer being there," one FBI agent said.

The Computer Analysis and Response Team (CART) is a group within the FBI that solves computer crimes. CART forensic experts are able to find out when and how data files were created. They can gain access to passwords. They can even find files that have been deleted from computers.

More and more criminals are storing information about their crimes on computers. In one recent FBI case, more than 63 computers were involved. The FBI says that today about half of its cases require a computer forensics expert.

In 2001, a man was sentenced to nine years in prison for robbery. As evidence, investigators had copies of the robber's demand notes. These notes had been printed out from his laptop. Even though the man did not save the files, forensic experts were able to find the robbery notes on the computer.

Another case cracked by FBI computer experts was called Operation Bullpen. The FBI estimates that today, at least half of all autographed sports celebrity items are forged. In Operation Bullpen, 26 people were convicted of creating fake signatures on posters, trading cards, and baseballs. Where was the ultimate proof? Investigators found it on the criminals' computers.

Rules for presenting evidence in the computer **domain** are very strict. There are many **limitations** as to what is allowed in courts. Files stored on a computer are usually considered physical evidence.

There is also "nonphysical" evidence. For example, information can be **obtained** from the way evidence is stored electronically on a computer. Forensic computer experts have to **exert** great caution not to change anything in a computer as they check it.

The FBI says that there are four aspects to the successful **coordination** of computer forensic work. These aspects include:

- Identification
- Preservation
- Analysis
- Presentation

Making sure that the information can be **authenticated** is crucial in all four aspects. Interestingly, digital copies can be perfect. However, photocopies are not. A forensic computer expert makes a digital copy of a computer file onto a CD-ROM when investigating a crime. Then, that scientist works on the copy, not on the original. It is important to any case that the original be saved exactly as it was found. If there are any changes made to the original, the computer file can no longer be used as evidence.

Computer forensic experts need to know about "slack space," or where deleted files stay until they're written over. They also have to know about hex files, log files, read-only memory files, and other such files that are hidden from ordinary users. They need to have an instinct for when something isn't right.

In one case, the FBI discovered that stolen credit card numbers were being used to buy computer equipment from an online auction dealer. The computers of two Russian suspects were carefully examined by forensic experts. The hidden files they found provided evidence that the Russians were committing the fraud. The theft was stopped, and the company the Russian men were using to cheat people was put out of business.

All Kinds of Computer Mischief

Another kind of computer theft involves computer sabotage, or intentionally damaging a computer's hardware, programs, or files. When companies later realize that their computers are acting strangely, they may hire computer forensic experts. These experts study computer files and slack space on the computer hard drives of any suspects. In the year 2000, the FBI conducted a Computer Crime and Security Survey. The report was surprising. The computers of many businesses are sabotaged by angry former employees who want to get back at the companies.

Computer hackers who use their skills to steal money can cause chaos for private citizens, as well as for businesses. The cost of computer hacking is staggering. **According** to an expert at a company called iDefense, the "Love Letter" virus, which was spread around the world in the year 2000, was created by one hacker. The virus cost its victims between $4 and $10 billion in damaged files and lost work time.

Creating and transmitting a computer virus is a criminal act. The maximum penalty for this type of crime is ten years in prison and a fine.

VIRUS ALERT

Identity Theft and Other Cyber Crimes

Imagine opening your bills and seeing that you bought thousands of dollars worth of items. You took trips around the world, ate in fancy restaurants, and stayed in luxury hotels. The problem is, you never even left home!

Stolen credit card information is a scary outgrowth of the computer age. The U.S. Department of Justice is prosecuting more and more people nationwide for this crime. In the year 2003, an Ohio man was able to **obtain** ten credit cards using the name, social security number, and date of birth of a woman unknown to him. He succeeded in getting a large chain hardware store charge card in her name. Then, he bought more than $7,000 of merchandise on the charge card.

Cyber criminals who victimize Americans can certainly be found outside U.S. borders. A Russian businessman who frequently traveled between the United States and Russia was arrested by the FBI and sent to prison in the United States for four years. The Russian man had hacked into the computers of dozens of U.S. businesses to steal credit card information. He had also threatened to delete the data and destroy the computer systems of some businesses unless they paid him money. In total, the criminal stole $25 million. He was finally caught when he visited a U.S. computer company that was really an undercover FBI operation.

What happens at a crime scene when electronic devices are involved? The major rule is: "If it's on, leave it on. If it's off, leave it off. But photograph everything!"

Cyber detection involves a lot of different activities. First, investigators listen for any electronic noises a suspect computer might be making when it is found. They check if the computer is warm. They look for activity lights. They listen for whirring or clicking sounds. They see what devices are connected to the computer. Unfortunately, criminal activity can take place without a human in sight. Someone can be quite far away from a computer and still destroy the data a computer contains. The term *WiFi* refers to computer systems that are not physically linked by wires or that can be remotely controlled.

Investigators **coordinate** their efforts to uncover evidence. They collect any notebooks or papers near computer equipment because these may contain passwords or other codes. Telephone answering machines and caller ID (identification) devices may also hold important data. Investigators must **exert** great caution in handling electronic gadgets such as scanners, beepers, fax machines, and computerized handheld organizers. Again, they must be careful not to destroy important data.

This computer security expert, Tsutomu Shimomura, helped the FBI catch one of the most notorious computer criminals to date, Kevin Mitnick.

When it's cold and dry outside, static electricity is produced. Static electricity can damage electronically held data. Heat harms data, too. Plastic evidence bags can't be used to store computer parts because they also generate static electricity. Instead, investigators have to wrap evidence in special, antistatic plastic, or in paper.

Many everyday objects, such as audio speakers, can damage electronic evidence. The magnets police use to recover bomb evidence can harm computer data. Police must even keep the magnetic powders they use for fingerprint gathering away from electronics.

The field of computer forensics knows no **limitations** in the number and sophistication of crimes. In addition to identity theft, cyber crimes include stealing access to cell phones and pirating, or illegally copying, software. A recent FBI bulletin states that computers have changed how people relate to each other. However, it says, human nature is still the same. Some people will continue to find new ways of breaking the law.

Developing Fields in Forensics

It's an expanding world in the forensics business. One example of a developing new field is voice recognition. Voice recognition specialists are needed in certain cases such as when kidnappers make demands over a telephone. Voice recognition experts also help in identifying voices caught on videotape. The FBI regularly uses voice recognition to verify certain criminals who videotape themselves.

Being able to evaluate voices can be very helpful. The Psychological Stress Evaluator (PSE) has been used to study tremors in the voice that the human ear cannot hear, but that show up on voiceprint tapes. Experts say that they can tell whether or not someone is lying by studying the tremors in a person's voice.

Forensic experts can be accountants, architects, psychologists, psychiatrists, or engineers. They can be archaeologists, geologists, environmentalists, or people who study insects. They might be people who study how a fire got started and why it spread. Many forensic experts are medical examiners. These medical doctors perform autopsies on people who may have been victims of crimes. Some forensic scientists are even working in **coordination** with others to help save endangered species from criminal activity. They may catch poachers, or people who capture or kill endangered animals. Through their investigations of chemical compounds, forensic chemists can identify companies that put toxic substances into our waters or onto our lands.

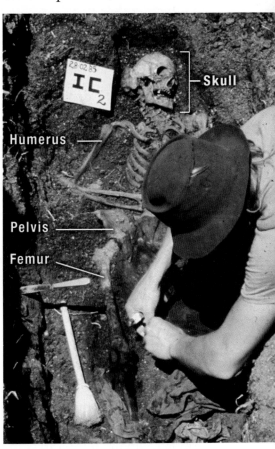

Not all forensic specialists work for police departments or the federal government. For example, many private companies hire computer forensic experts. These experts can help them safeguard their companies from viruses released by hackers, as well as from other computer attacks.

Most forensic specialists are hardworking and passionate about what they do. As one forensic specialist said, "You just can't beat a good mystery for pure satisfaction."

This forensic archaeologist is studying the bones of a possible crime victim.

CLUES from the LAB

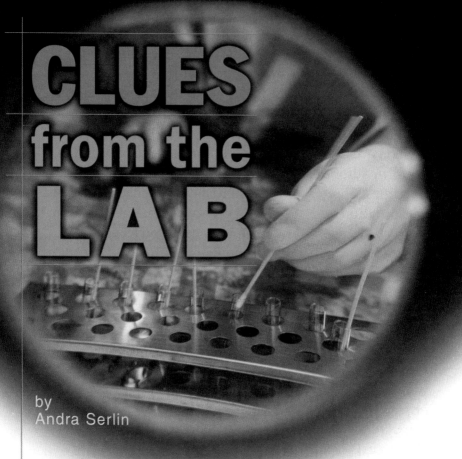

by
Andra Serlin

CHAPTER 1
Twenty-First-Century Detective Work

With a crackle of static, the radio at a police station springs to life. A criminal investigation is about to begin. A famous painting has been stolen. Detectives are needed to collect clues at the crime scene. A few minutes later, forensic detectives are speeding through the streets. Their job is to analyze the clues in a lab and find the evidence that will solve the crime. The skills they bring to the investigation are crucial to the outcome of the case. In fact, the crime scene will not even be touched until forensic experts arrive and take command.

Each day there are incidents that require the work of forensic detectives. Forensic detectives use science to unravel the details surrounding a crime. From fingerprints to voiceprints, DNA typing to handwriting analysis, there are many forensic science **achievements**. Forensics has become one of the most inventive ways to collect evidence. Forensics allows investigators to solve mysteries, both old and new. Advancements in forensic science have made it possible to **document** clues that have solved or shed light on thousands of crimes. Without DNA testing and other advanced methods used today, many of these mysteries may have gone unsolved forever.

Although forensic science most often deals with crimes, it can also help with scientific mysteries. For example, the extinction of the dinosaurs took place 65 million years ago. DNA studies might have been useful in finding out what caused the extinction. However, DNA from fossils more than 100,000 years old cannot be used. So scientists have to look for other evidence of an event that might have caused the dinosaurs to disappear from Earth.

In the 1980s, father-son physicists Luis and Walter Alvarez tried to explain the disappearance of dinosaurs. They suggested that an asteroid striking Earth from space could have wiped out the dinosaurs. They said that the impact caused an enormous cloud of dust to fill Earth's atmosphere. This dust cloud was so dense that it blocked the sun and killed most plants. The food chain from the smallest dinosaur to the largest was disrupted by the lack of plant life. The Alvarezes thought there might also have been devastating fires from an asteroid strike.

Although numerous theories have been made about the dinosaur extinctions, few have been proven by actual evidence. Was there evidence to support the asteroid theory? The Alvarezes believed the proof would soon be found. They made a formal **presentation** of their theory. A few years later, an impact crater about 65-million-years old and about the right size was found in Mexico. Scientists needed evidence showing that an asteroid had caused the crater. Forensic chemists tested samples of sediment and rock from the period when dinosaurs last roamed Earth. They found larger-than-normal amounts of the rare element iridium in the samples. They concluded that the iridium came from space—most likely from an asteroid. In other words, forensic science was used to find the iridium-rich "fingerprints" of an asteroid. These traces of the asteroid, along with the size and age of the crater, proved the Alvarezes' theory.

A *Tyrannosaurus rex* watches an approaching asteroid in this illustration. An asteroid's collision with Earth caused the extinction of dinosaurs, according to the Alvarezes.

CHAPTER 2

Forensics in Action

As you have just read, there are different types of forensic techniques, and the science of forensics relies heavily on testing. These tests can give us clues to what happened in the past, such as how civilizations lived. In this selection, you will read about some actual situations that involved forensics. In some of these situations, forensics was used to solve long-unanswered questions. In one case, evidence was discovered in the 1990s that gave information about an event that happened more than 5,000 years ago! Forensic scientists of the present were finally able to study clues about how people lived in the ancient past.

In addition to helping us **document** information about the distant past, forensics helps us uncover details about crimes of the recent past. "Cold," or closed, cases may now be reopened and solved well after a crime was committed. The reopening of cases is partly thanks to newly found scientific evidence that forensics provides. Evidence found by forensic scientists may help prove what law officials suspected, **notably** the innocence of suspects—or their guilt.

Some of the cases you will read about in this selection have never been completely solved. One such case involved the kidnapping of a baby in 1932. Mistakes made in the original investigation made it difficult to **confirm** a suspect's guilt.

Another case in which forensics was used was a tragedy that occurred about 30 years later, when a U.S. president was assassinated. Although forensics seems to have solved the case, some people still question whether the killer, who had Russian ties, acted alone or with others.

Other cases have been completely solved with the help of forensics. One of these cases took place in Russia in the early 1900s. The case had stumped investigators for years. It involved a woman who claimed that she was a surviving member of a royal family that had been executed.

One **similarity** between the Russian case and the final case you will read about in this selection is the subject of identity. A controversy about a man's true identity took place in the 1970s. It involved a crime about an autobiography. The book was said to have been approved by a famous man. You'll learn how the truth was discovered.

Criminal investigations today are helped greatly by the work of forensic experts. Debate continues over what kind of forensic evidence is considered "reliable" for use in a courtroom. Still, forensic testing is considered by all to be very important. Advanced methods of matching fingerprints or DNA show how far forensics has come. These forensic methods now help provide clues to great mysteries that had been unsolved before.

Researchers look at a DNA fingerprinting map at Columbia University in New York City.

Meet Otzi, the Ice Man

The date was 3300 BCE. The place was high in the mountains in an area called the Otztal Alps, between present-day Austria and Italy. That's where a man stopped to rest. A late spring storm had come upon him as he fled up into the mountains. Injured, alone, and in terrible pain, he knew his death was near.

The man was about 40 years old. Considered ancient by people of his time, he'd lived a good, long life. The man carefully laid down his bow and arrows that were covered with his enemies' blood. He removed his clothing. Then, clutching his favorite stone knife in his right hand, he sat down to wait for a death that was just hours away.

Fast forward approximately 5,300 years to September 19, 1991. Two German hikers traveling through the Alps spotted a man's body sticking out of some ice. The ice had preserved the body perfectly. It seemed as if there would be no problem in determining the identity of this unfortunate hiker who must have died from the frigid temperatures.

Soon the Alpine Rescue Service arrived. They began to dig the body out of the ice. However, this was not an easy task. Workers had to use a hammer and other tools to remove the body. It was wedged between two large chunks of ice. Four days later, on September 23, 1991, the body was finally freed from the ice.

The body pulled from the ice was that of a 5 foot, 4 inch tall male. Three layers of clothing made from grass and furs were found nearby. There were well-lined shoes, a cloak, a bearskin hat, and a belt. Some tools, **notably** a flint knife and a copper axe, were also found. It was this combination of clothing and tools that got workers thinking. It was quite possible that they were dealing with something other than a modern-day hiking accident.

A 5,000-year-old man, called Otzi, was discovered in the Alps of northern Italy by two hikers. A wooden backpack was one item found with the man.

The Mysterious Body

Scientists began to complete forensic tests on the mummified body. They were certain that Otzi, as they named the body, had not lived in recent times. Otzi lived in what is called Neolithic Europe, 5,300 years ago during the Stone Age. He had been perfectly preserved in the ice for all that time. His body was kept so well that scientists were able to determine where he came from, how he lived, what he ate for his last meal, and how he died. In fact Otzi, together with his clothes and tools, has changed the **prevailing** theories about our ancestors from long ago.

Otzi is so old that scientists have to be very careful about how they handle him. He is kept in cold storage at the temperature of 21 degrees Fahrenheit. To study Otzi,

forensic scientists may remove him from storage for no more than 11 minutes at a time. They must stay within this time limit in order to keep him well-preserved for future testing.

Although Otzi was found high in the Alps, he may not have lived there. Archaeologists wondered if he was a nomad who wandered around Europe or if he was from a local village. To figure out his origins, forensic chemists studied the **diverse** minerals found in Otzi's teeth and bones. The results were compared to minerals in the water and soil from all around the region where the body was discovered. The results showed that he was not a long-distance traveler. In fact, scientists believed that he had lived his entire life within a radius of 37 miles of where he was found.

Otzi's Last Meal

Forensic chemists also studied Otzi's hair. The results of the analysis indicated that he had an unusually high level of copper in his hair. His axe was also made of copper. Scientists concluded that Otzi must have made tools out of copper and stone and that he made the axe himself. This discovery forced researchers to reexamine a **prevailing** theory in science. Before examining Otzi, scientists had believed that the earliest humans started working with copper was more than 500 years after his death.

Otzi froze very soon after he died. Because he was so well preserved, forensic chemists were able to study the contents of his stomach, intestines, and colon. They wanted to find out about Otzi's very last meal. What they discovered helped them understand more about his life and death.

Otzi's last meal showed him to be a healthy eater. In fact, the wheat bread, green plant, and meat he ate about 8 hours before he died wasn't that much different from what many people eat today. Forensic scientists in Italy provided DNA **documentation** of the contents of Otzi's intestines. They learned that his last meal included ibex, a kind of wild goat, and a flat bread made from einkorn wheat. This kind of wheat does not grow in the wild in Europe. Scientists concluded that Otzi must have gotten the bread from a community where the people grew their own einkorn. Perhaps these people were Otzi's family and friends.

Also discovered in Otzi's intestines were microscopic bits of pollen. The pollen came from a hornbeam tree. Because this tree blooms between March and June in that part of Europe, scientists concluded that Otzi died in the springtime. He must have been immediately frozen by a late snowstorm that struck the area.

CHAPTER 3

The Ice Man's Final Hours

Scientists were excited about the discoveries they had made studying the contents of Otzi's stomach. They were able to learn a lot about the lifestyle of people who lived in those times. However, it was the cause of Otzi's death that really interested scientists.

When the Ice Man was first discovered, researchers believed that he most likely froze to death during a snowstorm. Another possibility was that Otzi may have been asleep when the weather changed. If a snowstorm hit quickly and unexpectedly during the night, he could have frozen to death before morning.

However, additional study of the ancient man led scientists to come up with a different theory about Otzi's last hours. They saw evidence of a man who was murdered or who had died after being wounded in a battle.

Notable molecular biologist Thomas Loy of Australia headed the forensic team investigating Otzi's death. The team was trying to **confirm** how he died. To begin their search for answers to this mystery, they thoroughly examined the body.

The first thing the researchers discovered was an arrow wound in Otzi's back. They asked themselves, "Did this wound lead to the man's death?" If so, then Otzi may have been the victim of an ancient murder.

This spear with a stone tip once belonged to Otzi.

One thing was puzzling about the arrow wound, however. The arrow shaft was missing. From the location of the arrowhead in Otzi's left shoulder, Dr. Loy concluded that Otzi could not have removed the shaft on his own. A new question then arose: Who did remove the arrow from Otzi's shoulder?

Further examination of the body led to more questions for forensic scientists. Dr. Loy's team next discovered that Otzi had cuts on his hands, wrists, and rib cage. These marks suggested to scientists that Otzi had been involved in some sort of battle right before he died.

Dr. Loy and his team wanted to learn more about these enemies who might have played a part in this ancient man's death. They wondered how many foes Otzi had. Did he fight a small group of men, or was he part of a large battle? Scientists believed that forensic science could play an important role in answering this question also.

To figure out what Otzi's last few hours might have been like, Dr. Loy's team conducted a careful search of all of the ancient clothing and tools. They were looking for any signs of DNA they could compare with Otzi's DNA. Close examination of the tips of his arrows showed that they had been used shortly before he died. Otzi's knife also showed signs of use, and a patch of dried blood was found on his cloak. Scientists used DNA typing to compare each of these samples with Otzi's DNA.

Tests performed on these new blood samples indicated that there were four additional strands of DNA that did not belong to Otzi. Two strands were found on one of Otzi's arrows. A third strand was found on his knife. The fourth strand of DNA was found on Otzi's cloak. Dr. Loy and his team now believed they had the **biological** evidence they needed to show that Otzi's death was not an accident but the result of his being in a fierce fight.

The location of the bloodstains containing DNA was important to scientists. Dr. Loy and his team used them to come up with a theory about what had happened to Otzi. "Presumably he was in a combat situation between 24 to 48 hours before he died," Dr. Loy said. "I think one of the things we could suggest is that he shot at least two different people with the same arrow. He retrieved his arrow each time." Dr. Loy's **simulation** of Otzi's fight explains how the DNA of two different people was found on just one of Otzi's arrows.

Researchers' discovery of Otzi's clothing and tools suggested that he was a hunter. With this knowledge, Dr. Loy speculated that Otzi was involved in a territorial dispute. He believed that Otzi strayed into another group's area and was involved in a fight with a few other people. Eventually, he was shot from behind while he was struggling with another person.

The final pieces of the mystery of what had happened to Otzi soon began to fall into place. At least two questions remained. Scientists wanted to learn more about the fourth strand of DNA. They also needed to figure out how the arrow shaft was removed from the hunter's back.

Remember that the fourth strand of DNA was found on Otzi's cloak. When they examined the entire cloak, researchers found that blood was on the part of his cloak that would have been around his shoulders. Researchers believe that Otzi must have had someone with him. If Otzi had carried his wounded friend on his back, then the location of this fourth strand of DNA makes sense. Scientists were able to, first, make the case for Otzi having a companion on his hunting trip. Then, they considered whether this person was the same one who had removed the arrow from Otzi's back.

Otzi's Companion

Researchers may never be able to completely **confirm** what happened to Otzi the Ice Man on the day that he died. However, forensic science has led to amazing discoveries about the ancient man and the times during which he lived. Otzi's body remains under strict supervision in a museum in Bolzano, Italy. Scientists continue to carefully study the body. They hope to gain even more insight into the past as more advanced methods of forensics become available. Every year there are more and more breakthroughs in DNA typing. Many other methods of testing are also being developed. Researchers believe that **prospective** scientists may soon have the chance to solve even more mysteries from the Stone Age.

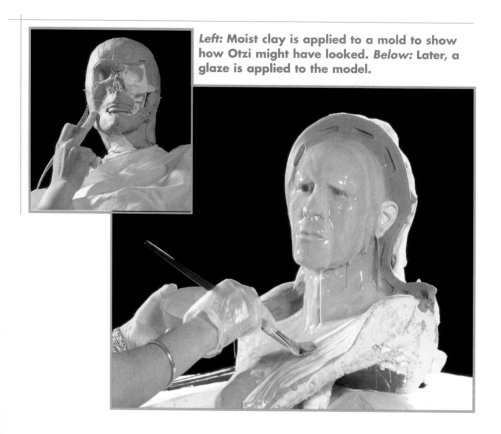

Left: Moist clay is applied to a mold to show how Otzi might have looked. *Below:* Later, a glaze is applied to the model.

CHAPTER 4
A Missing Princess

Not all mysteries are from the ancient past. The next mystery you will read happened in the year 1918. The place was Yekaterinburg, Siberia. On July 17, Nicholas Romanov, who was Czar Nicholas II of Russia, his wife Alexandra, and their five children were woken up in the middle of the night by armed guards. "Get dressed and come with us," the gruff military men told their former ruler.

Nicholas II and his family dressed and followed the guards to the basement of the house. What happened in that basement may never be fully known. It may remain a mystery that will puzzle people for decades to come.

Nicholas II, whose family had ruled Russia for more than 300 years, had been overthrown just months before that July night. Vladimir Lenin became the new leader of Russia. Many people think that during his **domination** of Russia, Lenin had ordered the death of the czar and his family. The guards were supposedly following Lenin's orders.

The sounds of shots rang out. Later that night, the guards informed Lenin that his orders had been carried out. Was it possible, though, that at least one family member had survived? That was the question facing forensic detectives more than 50 years later.

For many years after the death of the Romanov family, the government of Russia was reluctant to give out information about what had happened to Nicholas II and his family. However, just two years after the shooting, in 1920, a woman publicly claimed to be Anastasia, the czar's daughter. The woman lived in Berlin, Germany. Could forensic science **confirm** her identity?

Czar Nicholas II's children in 1910. Left to right: Tatiana, Anastasia (highlighted), Alexis, Maria, Olga

It was not until the 1990s—long after the death of the woman claiming to be the missing princess—that the mystery was solved. The investigation started with a search for the Romanov family's burial site.

Because the Russian government did not want anyone to pry into the case, finding the burial site was not an easy **achievement**. Geli Ryabov was a filmmaker who worked for the Russian government. Ryabov decided to investigate the **notorious** story. He somehow secretly gained access to government files about the Romanovs. In them, he found the name of the son of Yakov Yurovsky. Yurovsky was one of the guards who had been on duty the day the Romanovs were taken away.

Yurovsky's son gave Ryabov a note written by his father. The note revealed where the bodies of Czar Nicholas and his family were buried. To avoid being found out by the Russian government, Ryabov searched for the burial place at night. He located a site containing bones that turned out to be the remains of several people.

The remains Ryabov found were given to forensic scientists. Then, the work to establish whom the bones belonged to began. Scientists used special computer software. This software was used to compare the skulls to photographs of the czar and his family. The results indicated that the skulls had many **similarities** to those of the people in the photo. It seemed as if the Romanov family's burial place had been found.

Forensic scientists used DNA typing to obtain more proof that the bones were the Romanovs' remains. DNA profiling confirmed that the five skeletons were from one family consisting of a man, a woman, and three children. However, two Romanov children were still unaccounted for. Was it possible that Anastasia had survived?

More than 18 months after the apparent murder of the czar and his family, a woman jumped off a bridge in Berlin, Germany. She was pulled from the river and taken to a hospital. The woman had no identification, and at first, refused to say who she was.

After her recovery, the woman was sent to a psychiatric hospital. There, someone noticed her resemblance to the Romanovs. Information about this mysterious young woman was sent to members of the Russian royal family. These were family members who had escaped to Germany.

Eventually the woman, who now called herself Anna Anderson, did claim to be the missing Princess Anastasia. She claimed that one of the guards assigned to kill her family had saved her. Together they had escaped to Romania, and eventually, she ended up in Berlin. Anderson convinced many people of her claim to be the missing princess.

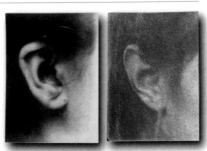

Anna Anderson   the real Anastasia

People who didn't believe Anna Anderson was Anastasia said her ears were different from the princess's.

Princess or Pauper?

Over the years, Anna Anderson spent time with living members of the czar's family. Some of them believed her story; some did not. After spending several days with Anderson, a cousin of Nicholas II exclaimed, "I have seen Nicky's daughter." On the other hand, Anastasia's former tutor called Anderson "a first-rate actress" after meeting with her.

In 1938, Anderson tried to claim Anastasia's inheritance and took her case to court to prove she was Anastasia. Expert witnesses were called to examine photographs of Anderson and Anastasia. Handwriting samples from both were analyzed. The experts seemed to agree that Anderson was the missing princess. The case dragged on until 1970. That year the court ruled that Anderson had not proven her case.

It wasn't until after Anderson's death in 1984 that DNA typing could be used to help settle this case. Experts compared hair and tissue samples from Anderson with the Romanovs' DNA. The results showed that Anderson was not the late Princess Anastasia. Instead, experts believed she was a Polish factory worker whose name was Franzisca Schanzkowska.

Schanzkowska had disappeared right before Anderson jumped off the bridge. Furthermore, **similarities** between the princess and the factory worker seemed explainable to forensic scientists. For example, Anderson had scars. She claimed that she received the scars on that fateful night when the czar and his family were killed. Scientists, however, suggested that the scars could have been caused by an accident at the factory where Schanzkowska worked.

Forensic science had proven that Anderson was not Anastasia. However, there are still people who believe Anderson's story. Why has the story been so memorable? Perhaps it is the romance of the tale—full of mystery and drama. It may still be **prevalent** because Anna Anderson's story is the one that many people prefer to believe.

CHAPTER 5

The Theft of the Eaglet

An even more recent mystery concerns an event that took place on March 1, 1932. The place was a mansion in Hopewell, New Jersey. On that cold and rainy night, a man approached. The ladder he carried had been skillfully modified. It was now long enough to reach even the highest windows of the large home.

Using only a small flashlight, the man circled around to the back of the house. He looked at the windows until he located the one he had in mind. Then, he carefully placed the ladder near the window and began climbing. Once inside the room, he grabbed a baby from the crib. Leaving a note on the windowsill, the man climbed down the ladder. He had just kidnapped the only child of a national hero. Reporters had nicknamed the baby "The Eaglet."

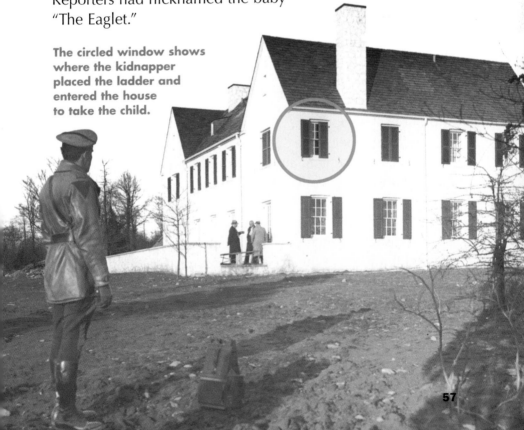

The circled window shows where the kidnapper placed the ladder and entered the house to take the child.

The kidnapping of 20-month-old Charles Lindbergh Jr. from his nursery was a crime that **dominated** the news. The crime shocked the nation. For months, detectives searched for the boy and his kidnappers. On May 12, 1932, the child's body was found in the woods only a few miles from the Hopewell mansion.

The Lone Eagle

Five years before the death of his young son, Charles Lindbergh had made history. In May 1927, Lindbergh was **notable** for being the first person to fly across the Atlantic Ocean alone. Lindbergh flew from New York to Paris in a small plane called the *Spirit of St. Louis*. He covered a distance of more than 3,500 miles.

Lindbergh's historic flight earned him the nation's highest award, the Congressional Medal of Honor. He was also given the Distinguished Flying Cross and the rank of Colonel in the Air Force Reserves. Lindbergh was honored as a hero, given the nickname of the Lone Eagle. The press followed Lindbergh everywhere. For a while, stories about him **dominated** the news. People were eager to hear about his every move. However, Lindbergh never liked the attention he received. He preferred to live his life quietly and out of the spotlight.

Lindbergh met Anne Spencer Morrow in Mexico, where her father was the U.S. ambassador. After the couple married and had a child, they built their house in Hopewell, New Jersey. They hoped it would shield them and their son from all the attention directed at them.

The disappearance of Charles Lindbergh Jr. was not noticed until late in the evening of March 1. Within 25 minutes, police officers were on the scene. They pointed out footprints under the nursery window. However, no one measured them, made a mold, or even took a picture of them. Other footprints were found inside the baby's room. These prints were not photographed either. Several yards from the house, the police discovered a long ladder divided into three **segments**. A chisel was nearby. When a local investigator arrived, he discovered the envelope by the windowsill that contained the ransom note.

Dear Sir!

Have 50.000$ bills redy 25.000$ in 20$ bills 15.000in 10$ bills and 10.000$ in 5$ bolls. After 2-4 days we will inform you were to deliver the Mony.

We warn you for making anyding public or for notify the polise the child is in gute care

This note shows evidence of a strange circular symbol appearing on all the kidnapping correspondence. Notice the errors in spelling and grammar.

In addition to the note, there was a strange symbol at the bottom of the paper. The symbol was a pattern of two interlocking circles with three punched holes. If this symbol appeared on any future correspondence, then the Lindberghs would know it was from the kidnappers.

Although this job was one for a forensics expert, this particular career had not yet evolved. Instead, police officers began work on the case by creating three very different and conflicting **profiles** of the criminals. The first theory was that the kidnappers were a group of professional criminals. According to the second theory, the criminals were local people. People who lived nearby may have known the location of the family's home and which window belonged to the child's room. The third theory suggested that it was an inside job, at least in part, by one of the Lindberghs' servants.

A week after the child was first taken from his room, a man named Dr. John Condon placed an ad in a newspaper. He offered his services as a go-between for the kidnappers and the Lindberghs. Both the Lindberghs and the kidnappers accepted Condon's offer. On April 2, more than a month after the child had been kidnapped, Lindbergh drove Condon to a cemetery in the Bronx, New York. Condon's job was to deliver the ransom money. The ransom was paid in gold certificates. Police officers had **documented** the serial numbers of the bills.

After driving Condon to the cemetery, Lindbergh waited for him in the car. Condon wandered around the cemetery for some time. Then, both Condon and Lindbergh heard a voice yell out, "Hey, Doctor! Over here." Condon walked to an area of the cemetery and met with the kidnapper. Both Condon and Lindbergh said later that the man had either a German or a Scandinavian accent. Condon handed over the ransom money. Afterwards, he received a note that showed the location of the baby. The note said that the boy would be found on a boat near the coast of Massachusetts.

However, the baby was not found until more than a month later. On May 12, a badly decomposed body of a young child was found about 4 miles from the Hopewell mansion. The body could not be positively identified, but an autopsy showed that it was **biologically** the same age as the Lindbergh baby. The autopsy also showed that the boy had been dead for several months.

Immediately after the child's body was found, the murder investigation began. Detectives **emphasized** the importance of three **diverse** pieces of evidence: the ladder, the ransom note, and the chisel. Also important was the ransom money given to the kidnapper. Investigators at the time really needed a break to find the people responsible for this gruesome crime.

CHAPTER 6

The Main Suspect

The big break came in September 1934. That's when a driver at a gas station paid for gas with a gold certificate. The gas station attendant wasn't used to seeing gold certificates, so he recorded the license plate number of the car. It turned out that the gold certificate that the driver used had been part of the ransom money. Police officers traced the license plate to Bruno Richard Hauptmann, a German immigrant.

Hauptmann was immediately moved to the top of the list of **prospective** suspects. He was later arrested, and police officers set to work finding the evidence to link him to the **notorious** crime. Two pieces of evidence, the ladder and the ransom money, would prove to be the strongest against him.

The ladder found at the scene of the crime had been professionally made. Later, it had been modified so that it could extend long enough to reach the baby's window. Police officers sent **segments** of the ladder to wood experts. One expert traced the wood used in the ladder to a lumber dealer in the Bronx, New York, near where Hauptmann lived. When police officers searched Hauptmann's house, they found the same lumber used in a **segment** of Hauptmann's attic. In addition, one of the floorboards from the attic was missing. Further testing determined that the missing wood from the attic fit the rails from the ladder perfectly.

The second piece of evidence was the ransom money. Police officers took apart Hauptmann's garage and found more than $14,000 of the ransom money hidden between the walls. Hauptmann told the officers that a business partner had given him the money as payment for some debts. However, police could never **confirm** the story because the business partner had died.

Two additional pieces of evidence were brought against Hauptmann in court. The first was Lindbergh's and Condon's recollection of Hauptmann's voice. Both claimed that his was the voice they heard in the cemetery yelling, "Hey, Doctor! Over here." However, Condon failed to pick Hauptmann out of a lineup as being the man he met and spoke to in the cemetery that night.

The final piece of evidence was the handwritten ransom note. No fingerprints had been found on the note or anywhere else at the crime scene. To tie the suspect to the crime, handwriting experts were called to testify at the trial. All of the witnesses for the prosecution, the party making the charge, claimed that Hauptmann's handwriting matched the writing in the ransom note perfectly. However, all of the witnesses for the defense claimed that the two handwriting samples were not a match.

A second ransom note was used as evidence in the handwriting analysis. The "B. H." might stand for Bruno H., leaving out his second name, Richard.

None of the evidence against Hauptmann—the ladder, the money, the voice, and the ransom note—could tie him directly to the crime. As the trial continued, everyone wondered what the verdict would be.

The trial of Bruno Richard Hauptmann dragged on for more than six weeks. The prosecutor assigned to the case **emphasized** the large amount of circumstantial evidence against Hauptmann. He included this evidence in a **presentation** that lasted for hours. His case suggested that this was a one-person kidnapping job that resulted in the murder of Charles A. Lindbergh Jr.

Hauptmann's personal attorney didn't do well for his client. Accounts of the trial paint a **profile** of Hauptmann's lawyer as an alcoholic who often fell asleep in the afternoon session of the court. Throughout the long trial, he spent fewer than 40 minutes alone with his client.

After 29 days in court, 162 witnesses, and 381 exhibits, the jury retired to the jury room to discuss the case. It didn't take them long to make a decision. On February 13, 1935, they returned to court with a decision. Bruno Richard Hauptmann was found guilty of murder. He received the death penalty for the murder of Charles A. Lindbergh Jr. The question forensic experts are still asking 70 years later is, Was he truly guilty?

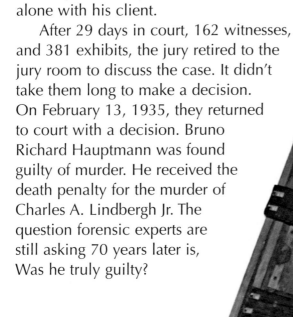

The kidnapper leaned this ladder against the Lindbergh baby's window.

Unanswered Questions

Some people now think it is impossible to know exactly what happened. Many think that investigators at the scene of the Lindbergh kidnapping made several mistakes. Some of today's forensic experts believe the wrong man was put to death for the crime.

The first mistake detectives made was they didn't close off the crime scene. Investigators, family members, and reporters all walked through it. They were not supervised, and they may have ruined some of the evidence.

You might remember that footprints were found at the crime scene. However, no mold was made, and no photographs or actual measurements of the prints were taken. Measurements might have tied the footprints to the suspect and **confirmed** his guilt or helped show that he was innocent.

There are also a number of unanswered questions. For example, how did the kidnapper know which window belonged to the baby's nursery? How did Hauptmann know how long a ladder would have to be to reach that window? Could one person really carry a ladder of that size?

Modern-day technology would undoubtedly have made significant **achievements** in this case. Forensic technology may have **confirmed** the identity of the kidnapper. Fingerprints might have been found in a DNA analysis. Also, tests of wood used in the ladder and in the floorboards of Hauptmann's attic might have revealed that they did not really match.

Unlike the earlier Lindbergh case, forensic experts are now called to the scene of a crime along with police officers. Yet, many unanswered questions can still remain. These questions are part of what makes the following story one of the most discussed crimes of all time.

CHAPTER 7

The Murder of a President

More than 30 years later, another **notorious** crime occurred far west of New Jersey in Dallas, Texas. The exact date was November 22, 1963. It was a beautiful day in Dallas, and crowds had gathered to watch the president's motorcade parade through the city. Many people were looking forward to seeing the young, handsome, and popular president. Cheering crowds greeted him, as everyone wanted to glimpse him and his beautiful wife.

One bystander had his eyes focused on the president's car. From high above the city, he watched the motorcade through the lens on his rifle. Moments later a shot rang out. In the car below, the president's hands moved to his neck. Another shot, and the president jerked forward. Secret Service agents rushed to the president's side and raced him to a hospital. Doctors did their best to save him, but it was too late. John Fitzgerald Kennedy, the thirty-fifth president of the United States, was dead at the age of 45. Now it was up to forensic scientists to figure out who had committed this shocking crime.

This photo was taken moments before President John F. Kennedy was shot in Dallas, Texas, in 1963.

Capturing a Criminal

While doctors tried to save President Kennedy's life, Secret Service agents and police officers did their best to create the shooter's **profile** and help them nab the suspect. Profiling the suspect is one of the first steps trained forensic professionals take. At the scene of the crime, police officers and Secret Service agents tried to find the shooter. They quickly interviewed witnesses to find out from where the shots had come. It didn't take long for them to turn their attention in one direction.

The first to arrive at the suspected scene of the crime was Dallas police officer Marrion Baker. Baker was a part of the presidential motorcade. His motorcycle was several cars behind the president's when the shots rang out. Baker looked to see from where they might have come. He noticed birds flying away from a window of a building belonging to the Texas School Book Depository. He dashed to the building and up the stairs. On the second floor landing, he spotted a man heading into the lunchroom. It was less than 2 minutes after the shooting.

One Main Suspect

Baker called to the man to stop. Even though the man originally looked suspicious to Baker, he saw that the man was empty-handed. Since Baker also saw that the man was a company employee, he allowed him to proceed. Later, when co-workers described this man, they would **emphasize** that he was "quiet" and "a loner." The man would become the main suspect in the assassination. His name was Lee Harvey Oswald.

Meanwhile, other police officers had arrived and began a search of the Texas School Book Depository building. On the top floor they discovered three empty cartridge cases. Boxes were set up that would be able to shield a shooter from anyone looking up at the building. Other boxes were arranged to give a shooter a secure place to rest a weapon. Nearby, officers found a bolt-action rifle with a lens for telescopic sight.

Police officers with forensic know-how sealed the floor. They ordered that no one be permitted to leave the building. The rifle was not touched until it could be photographed. Police officers began questioning everyone in the building, and when Lee Harvey Oswald was noticed as missing, officers were sent to find him.

Minutes after being spotted by Officer Baker, Lee Harvey Oswald was seen leaving the Texas School Book Depository building. Fourteen minutes later Oswald took part in another shooting, and 15 minutes after that the Texas police had him in custody.

The distance from the circled window, where the shooter perched, to the "X" on the street, where the president was hit, is more than a hundred feet.

As a child, Oswald had been diagnosed with severe emotional problems. As an adult, he had tried to defect to the Soviet Union. He tried this at a time when relations between the United States and the Soviet Union were strained. Oswald's political beliefs were very different from President Kennedy's policies. To the Secret Service, Oswald seemed to be the one and only natural suspect.

A Curious Turn of Events

After Oswald was arrested, he was taken to the nearest police station. When questioned, he denied any involvement in the shooting of the president. However, officers were sure they had their man. Now it would be up to a jury to decide Oswald's fate.

At 1:30 a.m. on November 23, 1963, Oswald was formally charged with the assassination of President Kennedy. On November 24, Oswald was to be transferred from the city jail to the Dallas County jail. Television, radio, and newspaper reporters were allowed to witness the transfer, and the room was crowded with people. As Oswald, flanked by police officers, came down a ramp toward a police car, a man suddenly stepped out of the crowd. In front of millions of television viewers, this man, Jack Ruby, shot Lee Harvey Oswald to death.

With Oswald dead, rumors began to spread that President Kennedy had been killed by more than one person. Some believed that Soviet spies had killed the president. Others thought that organized crime bosses had something to do with it. A few placed the blame inside Kennedy's administration, among those who didn't like the president's policies. Only the most modern forensic science had the techniques to prove to the world that Lee Harvey Oswald, acting alone, was responsible for the murder of the thirty-fifth president of the United States.

CHAPTER 8

Finding the Evidence

To government investigators and forensic scientists, the large amount of evidence made it clear: Lee Harvey Oswald was the lone assassin. From the evidence found at the Texas School Book Depository, it also seemed clear that the shots that killed the president were fired from the sixth floor of the building. Forensic scientists believe they gathered enough evidence to prove to the world that this was the truth behind the assassination.

However, rumors of a conspiracy were still around. To help in the investigation, a government commission was created soon after the assassination to look carefully into the crime. It was the job of the Warren Commission to gather all the evidence in the case and make a full **presentation** both to government officials and to the people of the United States.

In order to disprove conspiracy theories being passed from person to person, forensic experts working for the Warren Commission tested each theory. They compared the theory with the evidence found at the crime scene. In each case, forensics was able to account for the evidence that was found.

Anatomy of a Crime

The first and most-widely argued theory was that there were more than three shots fired at the president. Another part of this theory was that the shots came from more than one direction. For conspiracy believers, the existence of more shots would prove that Oswald was not acting alone.

Witnesses at the scene could not agree on what they had seen and heard. When the assassination took place, witnesses gave conflicting reports about the shooting. While most people reported that they had heard three shots all coming from the same direction, the direction of the Texas School Book Depository building, other witnesses thought at least one shot came from a grassy knoll nearby. Immediately after the shooting, police officers and witnesses ran up the grassy embankment to search the area. However, no person, gun, or bullet casings were ever found on the grassy area. According to the Warren Commission report, the three bullet casings found on the sixth floor of the Texas Book Depository matched the three bullets found at the crime scene.

Forensic tests of the bullets matched them to the rifle found in the building. Records obtained by detectives from the gun manufacturer also showed that Lee Harvey Oswald had bought the gun. According to Oswald's wife, it was in his possession up until the day of the shooting. Forensic evidence and basic detective practices worked together in this case to show that only three shots were fired, all from the same direction.

A second mystery for forensic science to solve involved the number of wounds the president received. Only three shots were fired that day, but President Kennedy and Texas

THE FORENSIC COUNT-UP

NUMBER OF		
	shots fired	3
	bullet casings found	3
	total wounds	7
	President Kennedy's wounds	3
	Governor Connally's wounds	4
	shots witnesses reportedly heard	3

governor John Connally, who was also wounded in the shooting, had seven wounds between them. Could forensics explain how this was possible?

According to a computer analysis using three-dimensional graphics, it is possible for a single bullet to cause multiple wounds. By looking at each **segment** of the computer images, forensic experts showed how a bullet could bounce from one part of a body to another. Experts believe that this is what happened to Governor Connally.

The governor was hit by one bullet. This bullet, shot from above, traveled in a downward-angled path. The bullet entered the right side of his body and exited the left side of his body. It hit his back first, traveled down through his chest and passed through his right wrist. Then the bullet entered his left thigh. Luckily, Governor Connally survived the assassination attempt.

A third conspiracy theory that was presented focused on President Kennedy's movements. At the second the shot hit the president, a film was being taken by a cameraperson. This film clearly shows the president's head moving backward as the shot hit him. Conspiracy theorists believe that this backward movement was caused by an additional bullet that came from the front of the presidential limousine. What could forensics tell us about this?

After the president was pronounced dead, his body was flown to the National Naval Medical Center in Bethesda, Maryland. Medical experts would need to analyze his wounds. The autopsy of President Kennedy was performed immediately.

A large head wound and an additional wound in the base of Kennedy's neck had been noted in the autopsy report. The autopsy notes say that both of these wounds are "presumably of exit." This means that they show where the bullets left Kennedy's body. The autopsy notes also discuss a small wound in the base of Kennedy's skull and another small wound in his head.

The doctors performing the autopsy reported the cause of death as "Gunshot wound, head." From the appearance of the wounds, it was clear to the forensic scientists that the shots came from "a point behind and somewhat above" the president's head. Forensic experts know how to trace the direction gunshots take and what kind of damage they create. Now, they could, again, provide insight into what really happened to President Kennedy.

In addition to the previous visual evidence, new forensic evidence has contributed to our understanding of the case. This evidence, based on the film that was taken, is a sound recording that some people say proves that there were only three gunshots. This newer evidence, again, rules out the first conspiracy theory.

Like the other conspiracy theories surrounding this case, three arguments originally made could all be ruled out by forensic evidence. Forensic scientists used **simulations** with computers and recordings to duplicate conditions of the shooting. These and other methods helped forensic scientists make important discoveries in this historic case. After seeing forensic proof, most U.S. citizens now believe that President Kennedy's assassination was the work of one individual, Lee Harvey Oswald.

Oswald's shots from the sixth floor of the Texas School Book Depository may have changed history. Yet thanks to forensic science, we have learned what actually happened on that fateful day in November of 1963. It was a case that, although mysterious, could be solved by the hard-working detectives assigned to it.

As you read above, forensic analysis of sound can sometimes help in solving a case. In the next case, you'll read about how sound was critical to finding a solution.

CHAPTER 9

Will the Real Howard Hughes Please Stand Up?

The date was January 1971. The place was the offices of McGraw-Hill, a publishing company in New York City. A man named Clifford Irving walked into the building carrying letters he claimed were written by an eccentric billionaire. According to the letters, Irving had permission to write an account of the billionaire's life.

Billionaire Howard Hughes was a movie producer and a famous pilot before he disappeared from public life. Hughes had isolated himself in a hotel in the Bahamas more than a year earlier and had not been heard from since. McGraw-Hill publishers knew the public was extremely interested in Hughes's life.

Irving showed the letters to the publishers. He wanted to prove his claim that he had permission to be Hughes's ghostwriter, a person who writes for another person. Were the letters real, stating that Irving had the go-ahead from Hughes for the book? If so, the book about the billionaire's life was sure to be a bestseller. Both the writer and the publishing company could make a fortune.

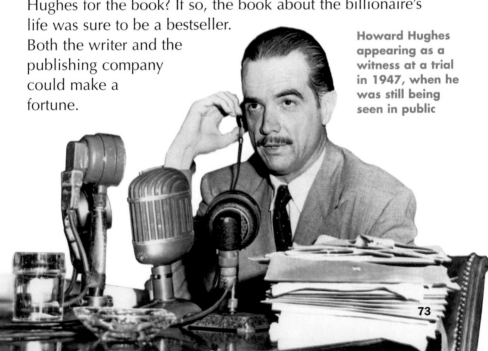

Howard Hughes appearing as a witness at a trial in 1947, when he was still being seen in public

McGraw-Hill immediately paid more than $700,000 for the right to publish the book. Legal documents needed to be signed between the publisher and Hughes. Irving forged Hughes's name, signing the legal documents as if he were really Hughes. McGraw-Hill gave Irving $100,000 as an advance, or up-front money. The publisher also wrote out checks totaling more than $600,000 that were supposed to go to Hughes. However, the publisher had no idea that the checks would be cashed by someone other than Hughes.

Irving quickly wrote and turned in a 1,200-page manuscript, and it was submitted for publication. Then, the scam was revealed.

It didn't take long for Howard Hughes to find out that Irving was writing a book about his life. Hughes telephoned a reporter who had been the last person to interview him. He told the reporter that the book, claiming to include interviews with Hughes, was a fake.

The reporter, Frank McCulloch, wasn't sure that the voice on the line belonged to Hughes. McCulloch decided to do some research. He got a copy of the manuscript. After reading it, he concluded that it was accurate. He based his opinion on the descriptions of Hughes. He believed some of the information in the book would have been available only to someone who knew the man. McCulloch determined that the voice on the telephone was that of an impostor.

After McCulloch gave his support to the book, Hughes made arrangements to have a conference call with several reporters. The reporters were allowed to ask Hughes about anything. Hughes believed that if he were able to answer all the questions there would be no doubt as to his identity.

The conference call took place on January 7, 1972. Seven reporters were present at the event. It was the first time that Hughes had come out of hiding in more than 14 years. During the conference call, reporters asked Hughes many personal questions, and Hughes answered them all. He **emphasized** that he had not given permission for this book to be written. He told reporters that he didn't know Irving. The reporters were convinced that the man on the telephone was Hughes.

Even though Hughes answered all the questions, the publishing company did not think that the conference call was enough proof to establish Hughes's identity. Irving insisted that the man on the telephone was an impostor, and many people believed Irving. McGraw-Hill decided to publish the book. Whom could Hughes turn to for help?

Hughes decided that forensic science could be used to prove his identity. A voiceprint expert was hired to determine whether the voice on the telephone was Hughes's. The expert's first task was to find a recording that was known to be of Howard Hughes. Luckily, the billionaire had given a speech that had been recorded 30 years earlier. This voice recording was exactly what the expert needed.

After comparing the conference call and the speech recording, the voiceprint expert was able to draw a conclusion. To compare the voices, the expert used a spectrograph, a tool that had just been invented. A spectrograph uses a chart to measure elements of the voice including pitch, tone, and volume. The expert compared a spectrograph of the voice in the speech with the one in the telephone call. It seemed clear that the voice on the telephone and the one from 30 years before belonged to the same person.

After the **confirmation** of the voiceprint, there was another discovery. Irving's wife had already cashed checks that McGraw-Hill made out to Hughes.

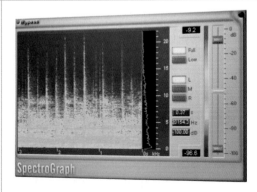

This tool, called a spectrograph, is like a lie detector for people's voices.

Real-Life Detective Work

To make matters worse, Irving had claimed to be interviewing Hughes. Irving was forced to admit that he had faked the story since he had never met Hughes. His manuscript had been based on the stolen manuscript of a long-time associate of Hughes's, who was hoping to publish his own version of the billionaire's life. Irving was found guilty of forgery and was sentenced to nearly 3 years in prison.

Like the other cases in this selection, the attempted forgery of Howard Hughes's autobiography was a mystery to be solved by forensic scientists. Only the techniques developed over the last 50 years have allowed investigators to achieve a clear and provable conclusion in many cases.

Without forensic science, important scientific information about the Ice Man might have remained a mystery. Today, we would know much less about the Lindbergh kidnapping and the murder of a beloved president. The woman who claimed to be a missing princess might have gotten away with her claim.

As you have seen, there are many **diverse** cases helped by the field of forensics. Science has come a long way toward helping to solve crimes and mysteries. Forensic investigators can now often **confirm** the identity of suspects.

Forensic scientists can also **simulate** what happened during a crime. The tiniest bits of **biological** evidence can lead to the arrest of a kidnapper. DNA typing can help nab a murderer.

Whether it's proving someone's true identity or unveiling the truth about how a crime was committed, forensics helps make important information available to investigators and courtrooms. For those of you who might be **prospective** forensic scientists, you will find many exciting career opportunities ahead. Maybe the next famous crime will be yours to help solve!

Glossary

accordingly therefore, or so. **According to** means depending on.

achievement the result of doing something successfully; something done by skill, work, or courage

administer to bring into use or operation

authentic trustworthy; genuine. Something that has been **authenticated** has been proven to be genuine.

biological having to do with the study of living things and the way they live. If two people are **biologically** related, they are blood relatives.

clarify to make clear or easier to understand

confirm to prove to be true. **Confirmation** is proof that something is true.

consistent agreeing; the same every time. **Inconsistencies** are things that do not agree with each other.

coordinate to place in proper order or relationship; to plan or invent. A **coordinator** makes things work together. **Coordination** is the act of working together smoothly.

devise to come up with; to invent or create

disperse to scatter in different directions or to distribute widely

diverse different or varied

document to write or print on paper information that may later be used as evidence or proof in an investigation. **Documentation** is printed information or proof.

domain a sphere of action or knowledge

domination the act of ruling over something or someone. **Dominated** means controlled or ruled, or made most important or powerful.

emphasize to give special force or attention to; to stress

exert to put into forceful action. **Exertion** is the act of working hard.

factual based on actual or real events

limitations restrictions

lingering remaining or staying longer

notable worth noticing or paying attention to. **Notably** means with attention to.

notorious well-known, especially for having done something bad

obtain get

pivotal extremely important; crucial

presentation the act of making something known or putting something on view publicly

prevailing having great force or influence; strongest; most common. If something is **prevalent**, it is widely accepted or believed to be factual.

productive giving good or useful results

profile a short biography; a graph or summary giving facts about a particular subject

prospective likely to be or become in the future; expected

segment any of the parts into which something can be divided or can be separated

similarity likeness; the condition of being almost, but not exactly, the same

simulation a recreation of an event. To **simulate** is to recreate.

Index